I Will Never Leave You

My Presence Will Always Sustain You

Mary Marriot

Mary Marriot

Kingdom Publishers

www.kingdompublishers.co.uk

I will Never Leave You

Copyright© Mary Marriot

All rights reserved. No part of this book may be reproduced in any form by photocopying or any electronic or mechanical means, including information storage or retrieval systems, without permission in writing from both the copyright owner and the publisher of the book. The right of to be identified as the author of this work has been asserted by him in accordance with the Copyright, Designs and Patents Act 1988 and any subsequent amendments thereto.
A catalogue record for this book is available from the British Library.

All Scripture Quotations have been taken from New International Version

ISBN: 978-1-911697-56-5

1st Edition by Kingdom Publishers
Kingdom Publishers
London, UK.

You can purchase copies of this book from any leading bookstore or email
contact@kingdompublishers.co.uk

Mary Marriot

All verses are taken from the
NKJV version of the Bible

Mary Marriot

Dedicated to the Glory of God

Mary Marriot

This short book is written for all Christians, having in mind particularly young adults, who, having left behind their childhood, are having to cope with the human metamorphosis into adulthood, an age which quite often is not understood by the older generations.

However, if young people are fed on the Word of God, life gives them a different ride, one that will strengthen, encourage and lift their spirits, allowing them to be appreciated as well as securing more understanding of their seniors.

Having a living faith is an enormous privilege, one which enhances all Christians in their walk with Jesus, and my hope and prayer is that all readers will be encouraged by reading 'I Will Never Leave You.'

The reader will find repetition in verses, beliefs and thoughts throughout – this is to bring emphasis on the narrative in hand, clarifying that which the Holy Spirit is saying overall. It is written with His guidance and in obedience to His request to write.

Mary Marriot

Contents

The New Birth	13
Jesus Encourages Us Every Day	15
The Healing Love Of Jesus	25
The Breaking Of Bread	33
Jesus Forgives Us	35
The Ten Commandments	43
The Importance Of Praise And Prayer	47
Facing Up To And Handling Pressure	51
The Way The Truth And The Life	57
Jesus In The Twenty First Century	61
Do Not Lie	67
My Thoughts Are Not Your Thoughts Nor Are Your Ways My Ways	93
Choose Today Whom You Will Serve	97
There Is Something Very Seriously Wrong	109

Mary Marriot

Chapter 1
THE NEW BIRTH

It is important that we all know about the 'New Birth' and how it takes place in our lives. When we are 'born again', we are able to understand, through the power of the Holy Spirit, God's written word. Without it, we do not have spiritual discernment – it is impossible, as God's Word is profound and unworldly.

John's Gospel 3:1-16 enlightens us to this fact.

Nicodemus was a secret follower of Jesus, and being curious, went to see Him at night, telling Him that himself and others knew that He was a teacher from God, otherwise what He did could not be done. Jesus replied that he would have to be born again in order to see the Kingdom of God.

One can imagine Nicodemus reacting the way he did! It didn't make sense, and he said so. Jesus went on to explain the whys and wherefores, but it doesn't say whether Nicodemus came into an understanding. However, in John 19:39 we read that he brought a mixture of myrrh and aloes for the Lord's burial. Perhaps this is telling us that he believed and was reborn?

So before threading your way through this short book, it is suggested that you read all about the new birth and if you haven't experienced it, maybe now is the time for you to do so.

Chapter 2
JESUS ENCOURAGES US EVERY DAY

Before Jesus left the earth to return to His Father in heaven, He made a promise that He would always be with us. And so He is, every second of each day, He lives in our hearts by His Holy Spirit.

In order to understand this, you will have had to invite Him to live in your heart and say sorry for the times you might have said or done wrong things. If you have done this, you will know what it is to be a child of God.

We are going to go through a few Bible stories, so as to encourage you in your walk with Jesus, and start with **John's Gospel Chapter 14:16-18. If you love me, keep my commandments. And I will pray to the Father, and He will give you another Helper, that He may abide with you forever, even the Spirit of truth, whom the world cannot receive, because it neither sees Him nor knows Him, but you know Him for He dwells with you and will be in you. I will not leave you orphans. I will come to you.**

It would be a good idea to have your Bible with you as you read through the book. Apart from the story telling, it can be a Bible study of sorts. You might have a different translation than the one used here, but the meaning is the same.

Who is this other 'Helper' Jesus mentions? He is our Comforter, the Holy Spirit, who lives within us, guiding us, keeping us safe and talks to us as a friend. To be able to believe this, we need to trust in God's word, and when we trust, our faith is alive and believing just happens.

Proverb 3:5-8 Trust in the Lord with all your heart, And lean not on your own understanding; in all your ways acknowledge Him, and He shall direct your paths. Do not be wise in your own eyes; fear the Lord and depart from evil. It will be health to your flesh, and strength to your bones. Trusting in the Lord takes faith, and not to rely on what we think we know, can keep us humble and totally reliant on Him who knows all. He is a faithful God.

The story of Jesus walking on the water we find in **John 6:16-21 And when evening came, His disciples** went down to the sea, got into the boat, and set over the sea towards Capernaum. And it was now dark, and Jesus had not come to them. Then the sea arose because a great wind was blowing. So when they had rowed about three or four miles, they saw Jesus walking on the sea and drawing near the boat, and they were afraid. But He said to them, "It is I; do not be afraid;" Then they willingly received Him into the boat, and immediately the boat was at the land where they were going.

These verses are telling us not to be afraid. Jesus says to the men that it is Him, and to trust Him in the storm; He said that He would always be with them, and so He was, despite their fears.

We all have 'storms' in our lives, when things don't go right; we may be upset over something with which we are unable to deal; we may have fallen out with a family member or a friend; perhaps problems with our studies. We need to take time out to sit with Jesus, tell Him all about it and leave it with Him to evaluate – remember we are not to rely on ourselves and our own understanding, but to trust Him.

There is an account in the Old Testament, which is known to be a favourite with many, even to those who do not believe in God. It is fascinating, and perhaps does sound rather exaggerated, but in God's world, nothing is impossible, and as it is in the Bible, it has to be true as the Bible is God's Word. **1 Samuel 17:1-57** Yes, it is long, so make yourself comfortable and read all about David and Goliath. (You might not want to read it in one session, but that's okay.) Then you can ask – where did David's courage and strength come from? - His Lord. So too, courage and strength come to us all from our Lord when we find ourselves in tricky situations. Let's hope we don't ever have to face a real Goliath! However, our circumstances may seem as big, but not to fear, keeping in mind that David went forward in the strength of the Lord, not his own. No doubt he didn't feel exactly strong in his humanity facing a man like Goliath, but His faith was 'in the name of the Lord of hosts', and he prevailed. Today remember the words of Jesus - **"I will never leave you."**

You may at times worry about what you are going to eat, or perhaps you would like some new clothes or shoes, or trainers, or even a new smartphone so as you are the same as everyone else, but there is not much available money. Let us take a look at **Luke's Gospel 12:20-21 And He said to His disciples, "Therefore I say to you, do not worry about your life, what you will eat, nor about the body, what you will put on. Life is more than food, and the body is more than clothing..."** Read on to Verse 34. Jesus is very explicit here, saying that there is no need to be concerned about the things that you think are important to have. His generosity always supplies all your needs. Notice the word 'needs' not 'wants'. There are times however, that He might give you unnecessary 'wants', even knowing that they are detrimental to you, just to show that His ways are best. Be always wise, and if wisdom is lacking, ask Him for it. **James 1:5** recommends this.

Are you embarrassed to talk about Jesus or do you love Him so much that you want to share your love and His love with others? Have you ever praised Him in song and dance? When King David was a shepherd boy, he was very musical; he played the flute and danced in front of others giving praise to His Father in heaven. Many people thought he was out of his mind, but David never cared what others thought. This can be found in 2 **Samuel 6:14.**

Psalm 23 is a beautiful song he wrote, and today, thousands of years later, is a favourite: **The Lord is my shepherd; I shall not want. He makes me to lie down in green pastures; He leads me beside still waters; He restores my soul. He leads me in the paths of righteousness for His name's sake. Yea, though I walk through the valley of the shadow of death, I will fear no evil; for You are with me, Your rod and Your staff, they comfort me. You prepare a table before me in the presence of my enemies; You anoint my head with oil; My cup runs over. Surely goodness and mercy shall follow me all the days of my life; And I will dwell in the house of the Lord for ever.** A song of total trust and faith!

A suggestion. In bed, before settling down for the night, read this Psalm, either aloud or to yourself, and then with your eyes closed, repeat the first two lines a few times before you go to sleep. In the morning, you might have a surprise. Try it and see!

There are so many verses in the Bible that encourage us to believe that He will never leave us. Choices had to be made in writing this book, as to write all of them would have taken forever, and it is not really necessary, as you can always search out the verses yourself. This would prove interesting, as you will always come across other verses that will catch your eye, and God may be speaking to you through these.

The next encouragement is taken from the book of **Daniel 5 and 6.** You may know this tale as well, as again, non-believers like it and find it exaggerated. But let us remind ourselves that -God is mighty and did (and still does) amazing things. The question to ask is why would a loving God allow Daniel, his faithful servant, to be put into a den full of hungry lions? The King, Nebuchadnezzar, ordered that he be put to death because he refused to obey him, and in those days people were punished severely for disobedience. (As was Adam and Eve who started all this!) Daniel wasn't a 'man pleaser'; he honoured and obeyed God by keeping His laws. We learn as we live our lives under God's laws, that it is always far better to obey

Him rather than man, reminding ourselves frequently that He will never leave us. God was with Daniel in the most fiercest circumstances.

Jeremiah 29:11 tells us that God knows what He is doing. - **For I know the thoughts that I think toward you, says the Lord, thoughts of peace and not of evil, to give you a future and a hope.** A very encouraging verse and good to hold on to.

There are times when we are all put to the test. Sometimes we have to choose between doing right or wrong, telling the truth or lies, obeying or disobeying. Doing right, being truthful, and being obedient are not always easy, depending of course on circumstances, but we need to know that God understands every minuscule thing that we are faced with each day.

God had greater plans for Daniel - as He does for you. God's ways are not our ways, nor His thoughts are our thoughts. Isaiah 55:8-9. **"My thoughts are not your thoughts, nor are your ways My ways," says the Lord.....**

Now, Jonah is an interesting character, and again we can read how, even though he was disobedient, God never left him, and forgave him for his disobedience.

If you are familiar with this narrative, then you know that he ended up in the belly of a whale (or a large fish). What a strange and awful place to be, and it seems ridiculous and certainly not possible. But it happened, and as Jonah says in his book **Jonah 2:2 "I cried to the Lord because of my affliction, and He answered me."** Continue reading up to **Verse 10** as it is all about God saving him. It is recommended to read all of this book. It has only four short chapters and it will give you a fuller understanding.

There are many more accounts throughout the Bible with regard to trusting the Lord. Paul, in the New Testament is a great example after his conversion to Christianity. If you seek these stories out, you will be greatly blessed. Paul wrote most of the New Testament, and you can read about him in the book of Acts, which is believed to be written by Luke.

Our breath is in His hands - just think about that - and though we have the joy of our salvation, we may often have to suffer for our beliefs, but always remember the words of Jesus, **"...and lo, I am always with you, even to the end of the age." Matthew 26:20.**

Chapter 3
THE HEALING LOVE OF JESUS

Jesus always heals, but not necessarily in the way we would like Him to, or expect. **Isaiah 53** in the Old Testament tells us about healing in our lives. It was written eight hundred years before Jesus died on the cross just for that – our healing in spirit, mind and body.

Verse 5. But He was wounded for our transgressions, He was bruised for our iniquities, the chastisement for our peace was upon Him, and by His stripes we are healed. Best to read the whole chapter.

What is this saying? Instead of ourselves being punished for the wrongs we do in this life, God sent Jesus to take our place. What we have to do, is to repent, that is, say that we are sorry for our misdeeds – nothing to it - but of course in sincerity. We are healed physically, mentally, emotionally and most importantly, spiritually, the last one meaning that we are made whole in our faith, our trust, our hope and our love for our Saviour.

We receive healing within, that is spiritually, and anyone who receives physical healing and healing from an illness are not favoured by God – it simply means that He knows best.

There is a Christian lady, who in 1967 was left paralysed after diving into a shallow bay. She was a teenager at the time and has been in a wheelchair ever since.

Over the years she has done, and is still doing, amazing works for other disabled people. At first she was cross with God for not healing her physically, but over time she came to accept that it wasn't His will for her to be healed this way.

She received tremendous healing within her spirit and has been an inspiring worker for Him ever since. She is a mouth artist, having painted normally before the accident. She thought that her ability to paint had been destroyed with her paralysis, but a nurse told her one day, that her gift to paint wasn't in her hands, but in her head and heart, thus she learnt to paint with the brush in her mouth. As soon as she accepted the paralysis, and changed her way of thinking, reuniting herself with Jesus, she ventured into her new way of life; the one God had planned for her.

Once again, we must remember that His ways are not our ways, and though we might not understand, if we accept this, we can move on. There are many mouth and foot artists in the world, Christian and non Christian, all gifted from God.

Physical healing is mentioned a lot in the New Testament, so let us have a look. **Matthew 8:2-3 And behold a leper came and worshipped Him, saying, "Lord, if you are willing, you can make me clean." Then Jesus put out His hand and touched him, saying, "I am willing, be cleansed." And immediately his leprosy was cleansed.**

On from there, Verses 5-9 A centurion asked Jesus to heal his sick servant by just saying the word, and Jesus said, **"Go your way; and as you have believed, so let it be done for you." And his servant was healed that same hour.** Read all the verses, breathing in the compassion of Jesus.

In the same **Chapter, Verse 14** we read that Peter's mother-in-law is sick in bed with a fever, and Jesus touched her; she got up and began to wait on Him. Later that day, crowds of people who were not well came to see Him and He healed them all. **Isaiah 53:4 tells us: Surely he has borne our griefs and carried our sorrows.**

In Mark's Gospel 7:32-35 Jesus heals a deaf man. Then they brought to Him one who was deaf and had an impediment in his speech and they begged Him to put His hand on him. And He took him aside from the multitude, and put His fingers in his ears, and He spat and touched his tongue. Then looking up to heaven, He sighed, and said to him, "Ephphatha," that is "Be opened." Immediately his ears were opened, and the impediment of his tongue was loosed and he spoke plainly.

Have you noticed that Jesus healed in different ways? Do you think it might be because we are all different and that He heals according to who we are and our individual temperaments? Maybe!

An interesting episode happens in **Luke's Gospel 17:17-19** (another leprosy cleansing.) Jesus was walking through a village **when He suddenly heard shouting. 'Jesus! Master! Take pity on us.'** They were the cries of ten men with Leprosy. All of them had been ostracised from the community and were obviously frantic. He told them to go and show themselves to the priests and on the way they were cleansed!

Only one man out of the ten returned to give thanks and glorify God for his healing.

Dissimilar again – and this is very important to note – only one went back to say thank you and to give God the glory. Having a thankful heart is of great value.

The last, but by no means the least, let us take a look at **Luke 5:17-25**. There was this wonderful occasion when friends of a paralysed man took him to Jesus for healing and they couldn't get into the house where He was, for there were crowds preventing them. They didn't give up, but opened up the roof and lowered him to the floor right in front of Jesus. When Jesus saw their faith He said to him, **"Man your sins are forgiven."**

By His stripes we are healed,
so His Word has revealed,
for He bore all our grief and our pain;
we considered Him smitten
and stricken by God,
He was wounded again and again.
Despised and rejected,
forsaken by men,
acquainted with grief
like a lamb He was slain;
wounded and bruised
for our guilt and our sin,
the needful chastisement
we placed upon Him.
By oppression and judgement

He was taken away,
a grave with the rich
we gave Him that day.
He committed no violence,
no crime – none at all,
but He gave of His life for us all.

It was the will of His Father
for His Son to die thus,
though righteous and upright,
a servant for us.
He bore all our ills
so the Word has revealed.
O yes, I believe
by His stripes we are healed.
(Taken from Isaiah 53)

Mary Marriot

Chapter 4
THE BREAKING OF BREAD
(Holy Communion, The Eucharist or The Last Supper)

Churches vary in the way the breaking of bread is prepared and shared, having selective titles as well, but ultimately each means the same. It is a reminder of the last time Jesus shared a meal with His disciples, and He wanted to leave a momentum for them and eventually the world. As He broke the bread and shared the wine He declared that the bread was His body, which would be broken for them and the wine was His blood which would be shed for them, and thus, after He was gone, they too, would break bread and drink wine in remembrance of Him and show the world to do the same.

We know that in partaking of the bread and wine we are eating and drinking spiritual food, a food which not only blesses us deeply, but is 'the living bread', essential for eternal life.

John 6:35 Jesus calls Himself 'the bread of life'. **"I am the bread of life; he who comes to Me will never hunger; he who believes in Me will never thirst."** And further down **Verse 51**

"I am the living bread which came down from heaven. If anyone eats of this bread, he will live for ever; and the bread that I shall give is My flesh, which I shall give for the life of the world."

You will read that many became angry, arguing as to how can they eat His flesh and drink His blood. In **Verse 63** He says "**It is the Spirit that gives life, the flesh profits nothing. The words that I speak to you are Spirit and they are life.**"

This sums it all up and gives us insight into what Jesus means. What gives life is God's Spirit. His words are Spirit and Truth, so His body and blood are spiritual food, thus partaking in the breaking of bread and wine brings us tremendous healing, comfort, peace and joy, and assures us of eternity.

It would prove to be worthwhile if you took time to read all of Chapter 6.

Chapter 5
JESUS FORGIVES US

"Forgive them Father, for they know not what they do." Luke 23:34. What extraordinary words, especially coming from someone who is dying an agonizing death on a cross, and being spat on and ridiculed whilst doing so. When Jesus was nailed to the cross many people stood looking at Him, some in silence, some were shouting at Him; some were crying and some were laughing. We know that His mother, Mary, was there and the disciple John. Jesus had been hanging on the cross for hours and not only was He in agony from the nails in His hands and feet and the thorns in His head, but also all the sins, diseases and guilt of everyone in the world. His pain and distress cannot really be imagined.

As He was nearing the end He knew that He had to forgive all the horrible people who had ordered His execution, plus all those who were taunting Him there at the very cross. Thus His words, **"Forgive them Father, for they know not what they do."**

We need to think about this when we have unforgiveness in our hearts, even down to the little every day gripes that might cause resentful feelings in us.

There are many situations in Scripture telling us of those who forgave and those who did not. And in society today there are the forgivers and unforgivers.

Matthew 6:9-13 "In this manner, therefore pray:
Our Father who art in heaven,
Hallowed be thy Name,
Thy Kingdom come,
Thy will be done
On earth as it is in heaven.
Give us this day our daily bread,
And forgive us our trespasses,
As we forgive those who trespass against us
And lead us not into temptation,
But deliver us from evil. Amen.

14. For if you forgive men their trespasses, your heavenly Father will also forgive you. But if you do not forgive men their trespass, neither will our Father forgive your trespasses."

If we say that we believe in Jesus, we know straight away that we must forgive those who hurt us. If we don't, then we are rejecting Him. It is not always easy, but we can do it with the help of God's Holy Spirit. Peter asks in **Matthew 18:21-22 "...Lord, how often shall my brother sin against me, and I forgive him? Up to seven times?" Jesus said to him, "I do not say to you, up to seven times, but up to seventy times seven..."** That is a lot of times. Do you think it is possible, let alone to forgive all those times, but to offend so often? Perhaps Jesus could mean a sin like murder, which to our way of thinking is insurmountable – how could we forgive someone who murdered someone we knew? Impossible! This is where we have to look to the cross and think of Jesus forgiving everyone in the entire world, and His taking the punishment for each one.

A well known and wonderful parable Jesus tells us, is the parable of the Prodigal Son, or the 'lost' son. The word 'prodigal' is explained in the Oxford dictionary as being 'recklessly wasteful or extravagant or lavish.' In reading about this in **Luke 15:15-32** we can learn a lot about forgiveness in an unstinting way.

When you have read it, think about the second son being resentful, the father being forgiving and the prodigal being sorry.

Let us see if we are able to recall a time, or times, when we have been unkind to someone, or someone has been unkind to us. How did we feel? Did we say we were sorry? Did the other person apologise, and if so did we accept it? What were our feelings and attitude before and after?

It is wise to question ourselves, as it helps us to think about wrong and right attitudes instead of skipping over them.

There are many, many people who have forgiven the most awful things done and said to them. Saints and martyrs of old, and even today, we hear of people forgiving the most outrageous actions wrought upon family or friends. But it is not only in extreme situations that we have to learn to forgive; we need to think about everyday circumstances where someone may have offended us. As already mentioned above, we need to question ourselves; children as well as adults can say and do nasty things to one another, to which there needs to be acknowledgement and apologies in order to live as Christians.

To be followers of Jesus costs. To 'cost' means that we quite often have to pay a price, which signifies that we must make sacrifices. This might be difficult, but if we look at it as putting the other person's feelings first, and even though we don't like the person, we have no right to offend her/him. So to make amends in a good way is a way of sacrificing bad feelings for good ones. If you see someone you don't like in trouble and obviously needing help, instead of ignoring the situation, go forward to offer a hand. This would be sacrificing your bad feelings for good, so being a friend instead of an enemy. The person might not like you either, but Jesus says to 'love your enemies'. We can find this in **Matthew 5 and Luke 6** under the title 'Love your Enemies'.

When you have been offended, you might feel you want to 'get your own back', but that is to be spiteful. 'Two wrongs don't make a right' is a phrase well worth remembering.

Many of us go to bed cross, and perhaps wake in the morning feeling unhappy and not in a good mood to face another day. That is because we allowed 'the sun to go down on our anger'. Paul says in **Ephesians 4:26 "Be angry, and do not sin, do not let the sun go down on your wrath, nor give place to the devil."** In other words, let us forgive one another before the day is over. Anger can lead us into sin and sin separates us from God. Always know, however, that He is ready to forgive us as soon as we are sorry. We are all accountable to the Lord for our own actions. There is no use blaming others for the wrongs we do ourselves and saying it was their fault for what we did. That doesn't hold anything with our Lord. Remember He knows us through and through and we cannot hide anything from Him. This has to be a pleasing thought, so we are able to be absolutely honest with Him. There is never any need to be afraid of His knowing our failings. He loves us and is always at hand to have a chat about anything. He is there to cry with us and laugh with us.

Psalm 139 is a unique Psalm to read on a regular basis, as it is so very encouraging.

Another encouraging read is **Proverbs 3**. It is a passage which gives tremendous advice to those who want to live the way God has called them to live. The Bible is our spiritual food, and the more we read it, the hungrier we will become. When we don't eat, we feel hungry, and we need to satisfy the hunger by having a meal. The same goes for spiritual hunger – His Word can only satisfy, and so we need constant nourishment from the Scriptures. He will never leave us or forsake us and so we are able to say (or sing!)

What a friend we have in Jesus,
all our sins and griefs to bear,
What a privilege to carry
everything to God in prayer.

Oh, what peace we often forfeit,
Oh, what needless pain we bear,
All because we do not carry
Everything to God in prayer.

Have we trials and temptations?
Is there trouble anywhere?
We should never be discouraged
Take it to the Lord in prayer.

Can we find a friend so faithful
Who will all our sorrows share?
Jesus knows our every weakness
Take it to the Lord in prayer.
(Written by Joseph M Scriven, 1820-1886)

Chapter 6
THE TEN COMMANDMENTS

We all know that there are rules in our homes and in society that are essential for our well being. And rules are made to keep, not break, though one often hears the joke that rules are made to break not keep! When they are broken it can cause problems, sometimes very serious ones.

There is a Highway Code, a set of traffic laws, to keep us safe on the roads. If we go through a red light, there could be serious consequences. If we exceed the speed limit, the same, and many more.

There are home rules as well, though of course there are differences, but rules nevertheless. You must be home at a certain time, no television at specific times and so on. To kick against them is pointless as this will make matters worse.

There are 'God Rules' - known as the Ten Commandments. These were given by God to Moses around 3,500 years ago. You might well think that rules that are so ancient must be redundant, but this is not the case. If you believe that God is the Creator of the world then you will also believe that His Ten Commandments were given to mankind to obey forever. Why? Because they make sense and keep us in good order, plus by obedience you honour God, just as you honour your parents and the law of land by keeping to their rules. This nation has gone head long into an abyss of destruction by doing away with rules that would help us to live honourable lives. His rules are there to keep everyone safe, and though we might often be tempted to break them, and possibly do so, (as with the home rules and laws of the land,) because we are defective human beings, God gives us the grace to repent and get ourselves in order again.

Unfortunately in today's world, we have run amok, doing as we please, breaking the Commandments, and most probably are not aware of doing so. The reason for us not being aware is because we are no longer taught the Commandments and many are ignorant of their existence.

It is about time awareness came back into our lives, else we will find ourselves not remaining in God's love. This is very serious.

Let us take a look at **John 15:10 "If you keep My Commandments, you will abide in My love, just as I have kept My Father's Commandments and abide in His love."**

The Ten Commandments are in the books of Exodus and Deuteronomy (Old Testament) and Jesus talks of them in the Gospels as mentioned above, as do some of the writers of the Epistles.

They are mentioned in **Romans 13:9** and **Ephesians 4:28** plus twelve other books. Instead of listing them here, it might be worthwhile to use this opportunity to have a project. – to look for the Commandments of God in the New Testament and see that they are far from being redundant. Plus you will come across other commandments which we are also obliged to keep.

Mary Marriot

Chapter 7
THE IMPORTANCE OF PRAISE AND PRAYER

We need to be aware of how important prayer and praise is in our daily lives. We know that God made us all in His image, nevertheless, we are all distinctive and unique. Because of this we pray and praise in various ways.

Foremost, we must adhere to the First Commandment, which as is written in these pages, is to love God first and above anything and anybody.

It is so good to give thanks to God – to thank Him for so much, even down to a glass of water. We need to go into our 'closets' as well to spend quiet times giving thanks for all we have. We must also listen to what He might want to say to us. It might be a word spoken quietly into our Spirits or from the Bible; He can speak to us anywhere at any time, and anyhow.

Some people pray for hours on end, maybe on their knees, sitting or lying down, but pray they do – these folk are called 'intercessors'. In other words, they make requests for others. Not everyone is called to pray this way. Many pray when they go to church or at a prayer meeting; others pray quietly in their hearts during their activities. Talking to God should come naturally, chatting with Him about friends, family, the sick, the dying, world situations, politics, leaders of nations, of churches and so on. This can be done whilst out walking, cooking, writing, lying in bed, sitting, even whilst listening to the radio or watching the television. We can be in constant contact with Him, He who is that all time friend and brother, even though He is a King. Maybe you know the beautiful song 'As the Deer', by the writer Martin J. Nystrom.

There was a lady, a nurse by profession, who, whilst watching the television one evening, heard the Lord in her Spirit say that she must go and look after a particular person, someone whom she had never met and wasn't a Christian. She obeyed and cared for this person for twelve years. Though she had been watching television, her Spirit was open to receive. No doubt there are many, many folk who have had similar callings, having learnt the art of having 'spiritual listening ears'.

We often do a lot of praying for this and that (all very important and special) and that is fine, but it is so vital to have quiet times as well. We have one mouth and two ears, so perhaps we need to listen twice as much as we speak!

Let us look at some verses with regard to praise. It is always better to praise God first before we pray. Somehow it seems the right thing to do. Many of the Psalms were written by David, as a shepherd boy, and when he was King of Israel. **Psalm 148** is a wonderful Psalm of Praise, as is **Psalm 147.**

But, we can use your own praise, remembering that praise is powerful as is prayer. Prayer in faith, as Jesus says, can move mountains. **Matthew 17:20.**

One thing though - we need to understand that everything is answered in His time zone, not ours. That might come as difficult to take on board. We think that we need, or want, immediate answers to something, but there is just silence. It is as though we haven't been heard. His silent response is not encouraging, but this is where we have to learn to trust that God knows best, and His timing is no other than perfect.

Prayers do not have to be long. Sometimes, perhaps most times, just a few words will suffice, and it is always good to give a 'thank you' on closing. It is not healthy to become bogged down with petitions, after all He already knows what we are going to say. Why then, we might ask, do we pray if He already knows everything we ask for? It keeps the doors of communication open and we all like to be with, and talk with those we love. He loves our company and always wants to listen to our requests.

It is good to give thanks to the Lord, to sing praises to Your name, O most high Psalm 92:1. There are also many songs and hymns which can be used as praise, either by singing or simply saying them.

Chapter 8
FACING UP TO AND HANDLING PRESSURE

Living in the digital generation for most, especially young adult Christians, is no easy thing. Lives are surrounded by everything technological and there is seemingly no let up. It seems that there is no choice but to be engaged with it – but, they do have a choice as to its usage.

Social media and all that it entails is very over-powering and somewhat demanding, insisting that we empower ourselves with all the 'know hows' and 'must haves'. If it could keep us awake all night, no doubt it would. It is addictive and very dangerous. Addictive because we are caught in the spider web - www (world wide web) or 666 which is the number of the beast in Hebrew and Greek. **Revelation 13**. There is no escape, unless, we seriously want to honour God and love Him above all else, then He is the way of escape as we read in **1 Corinthians 10:13. No temptation has overtaken you except such is** common to man; but God is faithful, who will not allow you to be tempted beyond what you are able, but with the temptation will also make the way of escape, that you may be able to bear it.

It is dangerous because Satan's gambit is to have everyone in hell. God doesn't use gambits, for He sent His Son Jesus to invite us to live with Him in heaven after our earthly life. He doesn't have to be crafty or sinister at all, but Satan does, so as to fool us into believing that the digital world is the essential part of our life.

As already mentioned, we have to accept that the multimedia world is here to stay, but again, as already stated, we have a choice as to its usage, and for this we need wisdom. (Repetition is to emphasise the importance of what is written.)

Proverbs 3 entitled 'Guidance for the Young' and **Proverbs 4** 'Security in Wisdom' make beneficial reading.

Ephesians 5:15-17 See then that you walk circumspectly, not as fools but as wise, redeeming the time, because the

days are evil. Therefore do not be unwise, but understand what the will of the Lord is.**

There are many verses in the Bible, New and Old Testament, on wisdom, and it would prove valuable to search them out. **Ecclesiastes,** written by King Solomon, is a recommended read.

Solomon, who was King David's son, was considered at some stage to be the wisest man that ever lived, thus his writings of twelve chapters. Unfortunately, he took his eyes away from God, and foolishly looked to the world. This so easily happens when tempted by Satan. Solomon's story is found in **1 Kings 3** where he requests wisdom, and then in **1 Kings 11** his downfall.

We all need to choose wisdom rather than foolishness and it is foolishness to follow the way of the world. It would be wise to ask the Lord how we are to interact in our own digital world and if we are serious in our requests, His Holy Spirit will guide us in this. Thus we will have that **'peace that passes all understanding' Philippines 4:7,** and we will cope with being different from those who think that we are weird. However, in all this, keep humble and teachable **James 4:10 Humble yourselves in the sight of the Lord, and He will lift you up. And Proverbs 19:20 Listen to advice and accept instruction, that you may gain wisdom in the future.**

And remember to pray for those who take the mickey. Jesus offers them salvation as well. It is better to be considered weird in this world and have eternal life than to go with the world and end up going to hell. Jesus says in **Matthew 5:29 "And if your right eye causes you to sin, pluck it out and cast it from you; for it is more profitable for you that one of your members perish, than for your whole body to be cast into hell."** This is a good example with regard to our choices in all walks of life and particularly the digital world.

It is imperative that we ask for wisdom concerning the company we keep. **1 Corinthians 15:33 Do not be deceived: Evil company corrupts good habits.**

From the time we were born God has been moulding us. Yes, from babyhood He has had His eye on each boy and girl, (though He knew us before we were born!) **Psalm 139** spells out God's knowledge of everyone. We might resist His guiding hand, wanting to go our own way, which of course is detrimental to our way of living. However, with His patience, He waits for our return, so that He can continue His moulding.

In **Jeremiah 18:1-11** He was speaking about Israel, a very disobedient nation. **Verse 6 "Can I not do with you as this potter?" says the Lord. "Look, as the clay is in the potter's hand, so are you in my hand, O house of Israel."** So too, we are in His hand, moulding us into His likeness - if we permit Him.

We need to always remember that Jesus said that He will never leave us. Even when we forsake Him, He anticipates our return, knowing that **There is no condemnation for those in Christ Jesus. Romans 8:1.** and **Verse 28 And we know that all things work together for good to those who love God, to those who are called according to His purpose.**

Mary Marriot

Chapter 9
THE WAY THE TRUTH AND THE LIFE

No one likes to appear different from their peers. This is understandable as it is very unpleasant being and feeling the odd one out. There is no way around this if you have decided to be a follower of Christ. Even Jesus Himself was considered radical, and so those who chose to go along with Him were considered strange by those who didn't.

Having a particular belief can hold one very steadfast, and this does not only apply to Christianity, but to other well known religions, theories, cults and much more. To alter that belief, one could be considered a traitor.

However, there is one extremely large difference, and that is that true Christians have the indwelling of the Holy Spirit. This is intrinsic to our nature from the moment we have given our lives to the Lord. We have an intimate, personal relationship with God through Jesus. It really is quite astonishing, and as we grow in our Christian life, we will realise more and more how very fortunate and extremely blessed we are to have been chosen by God to follow Him.

Matthew 4:19-20 Jesus bids the fishermen to 'follow Him'. These men were uneducated and rough, but Jesus saw their potential. No matter what stance in life we take, His love is equal for all, from the beggar to the Queen.

….And He said to them, "Follow me, and I will make you fishers of men." Then they immediately left their nets and followed Him. They wouldn't have known what He meant, nevertheless, they just dropped what they were doing and obeyed. Christ had a special aura about Him, and His voice must have been very intriguing! He spoke with authority as well, but not gruffly.

If we are to be followers of Jesus, obedience is a must, and to obey, at times, will cost. But know, the best and easiest way to have peace with what Jesus asks us to do, is to draw aside on our own and use those listening ears. It may take a little time, but eventually we will recognise His voice and on doing so, will know peace within our souls. To be still and know that He is God, He is sovereign, and He knows what is best is the finest assurance we can have.

"**Be still and know that I am God; I will be exalted among the nations, I will be exalted in the earth!" The Lord of hosts is with us; the God of Jacob is our refuge. Psalm 46.10.** It is in the stillness that we will hear, especially when we might be confused, annoyed, dismayed and many other negative emotions that pull at the heart strings.

1 Kings 19 tells us about Elijah when he escaped from Jezebel, running for his life; he went into the wilderness and sat down under a broom tree, praying that he might die. But God had things for Elijah to do, and it was here, eventually, when he had simmered down, that he heard God in 'a still small voice'. **Verses 11-13.**

It is imaginable to hear God speak in any situation, but more so if we are calm and not in a state of anxiety, like the nurse who was watching television at the time she heard God speaking in her spirit. Elijah had to rest and chill out first, then having done so, he became open to hearing that still quiet voice. God doesn't shout in order to have our attention. Think of how you feel when someone shouts at you to do something – it is not very pleasant and could possibly do more harm than good. **Proverbs 15:1 A gentle answer turns away wrath, but a harsh word stirs up anger.**

And Jesus tells us in **Matthew 11:29 "Take my yoke upon you, and learn from me, for I am gentle and lowly in heart, and you will find rest for your souls."**

Some people have tried finding the meaning to their lives by going with a specific cult or social movement, and they become hooked in their ways believing it to be 'the right way.' But do we ever wonder about them? Are they truly at peace and happy with their choice? Are we, as Christians, truly at peace and happy with our choice? Is there a significant difference? One learns in life that to argue with someone with regards to beliefs is pointless. To discuss differences can be healthy, just as long as it doesn't send you head long into fraying friendships. To pray for our unsaved friends is the best option, keep the peace at all times as much as it is possible and love them. Jesus died for them as well, and as Paul says in **1 Timothy 2:1-4 "Therefore I exhort first of all that supplications, prayers, intercessions, and giving thanks be made for all men, for kings and all who are in authority, that we may lead a quiet and peaceable life in all godliness and reverence. For this is good and acceptable in the sight of God our Saviour, who desires all men to be saved and to come to the knowledge of the truth."**

Chapter 10
JESUS IN THE TWENTY FIRST CENTURY

A strange thought! Have you ever considered what Jesus would be like now, living in the Middle East? Would He be wearing the same style of clothes and sandals? Would His hair be long? Would He be walking around with a smartphone? Would He be interested and involved in social media, the television, computers? Would He preach in churches, on the streets? What would He be like? Would He be the same as He was 2000 years ago? We can only guess the answers to these questions. One thing is for sure though, He was, and still would be a gentleman. He was, and still would be a good listener. He was, and still would be a good preacher. And as He spoke with authority then, He would do so today. And He would still be offering us salvation. **Jesus Christ is the same yesterday, today and forever. Hebrews 13:6-8.** Absolute certainty is that He would be exactly the same in character and personality. His teachings we read about in the Bible would be precisely the same, no change, no ifs and buts; what He said then, He would say today, in fact we know that His teachings still hold today by the indwelling of His Holy Spirit.

The smartphone is an interesting factor. Do you think He would use one? It has become part of our 'dress' and a 'can't do without' gadget, seemingly taking up most of our time. It appears Christians even use it in services, Bible studies and prayer groups – it is a 'must have.' Do you think Jesus would see it as an absolute necessity in our places of worship, prayer and study? If He still did carpentry, if He went from town to town, city to city preaching, would He carry a smartphone with Him, relying on it for information and various data? These questions may be difficult to answer, and perhaps make you smile, but they are worth thinking about.

We have become so caught up with technological devices that they have us addicted; what would He think?

Jesus had common sense; He was wise and He was holy. Feasibly we are blessed with common sense, but we are not always wise or holy. **1 Peter 1:15-16...but He who**

has called you is holy, you also be holy in your all your conduct, because it is written, "Be holy for I am holy."

If we attend church, Bible studies or prayer groups, we might, or might not use our smartphones, but presuming that we do, would we consider not using them and instead use a Bible? Living in the Western world we are hugely blessed with Christian book shops, which sell Bibles, as do well known secular book shops. The Bible isn't a distraction as is the smartphone. Texts and phone calls might register, both causing a disturbance during the study, prayer or service, unless of course the phone is switched off. Kept on silent, there is always the temptation to take a peak to see if anything has come through. Satan is a master at distraction, doing anything within his power to keep our minds and hearts muddied, instead of being tranquil and focused on the Lord. One of his tactics is to be a bluffer. We are so vulnerable, taken in by the things of the world that are set to destroy us. We need to be aware of his strategies, be shrewd with our choices in the use of the smartphone, and in all this, pray for enlightenment, and if one is sincere, God will see this and grant a welcome and helpful answer.

We are to honour God and worship Him alone. He must be supreme, not allowing anything else to stand in His way.

Jesus always honoured His Father. So too must we. Because social media is such an out and out distraction, it belies us into thinking that it is okay to use the phone as and when. Yes, perhaps so, as there isn't a law against it, and it does have a positive side – when used wisely. We need to know how to separate the positive from the negative, putting the phones aside in certain situations and bathe in the freedom that Jesus gives us – **Luke 4:18 The Spirit of the Lord is upon me, because he has anointed me to preach the gospel to the poor; he has sent me to heal the broken hearted, to preach deliverance to the captives and recovery of sight to the blind, to set at liberty those who are oppressed, to preach the acceptable year of the Lord.**

Isaiah 40:29-31 is very encouraging, and if you know anything about eagles you will understand its meaning:

He gives power to the weak, and to those who have no might He increases strength. Even the young men shall utterly fall, but those who wait on the Lord shall renew their strength; they shall mount up with wings like eagles, they shall run and not be weary, they shall walk and not faint.

It is recommended to read all of chapter 40.

Mary Marriot

Chapter 11
DO NOT LIE

Adam and Eve, unfortunately for us, did a few 'firsts', one of them being - they 'hid from God' - from him, not in Him. Why? Because they had disobeyed His Commandment not to eat of the Tree of Knowledge, and having done so they realised that they were naked, whereas up until then, being innocent, they were free in their nakedness; now they felt ashamed and embarrassed. **Genesis 3.**

We, too, think that we have to hide when we have done wrong, especially when it comes to telling lies, 'fibs' or 'white lies'. We fear punishment. Telling 'fibs' begins at a very young age, somehow it is an instinct within us, that if we fib, we might 'get away with it.' The word 'fib' isn't as strong as 'lie' as we think children are more innocent, but nevertheless, they hope that they will not be found out, and if this happens often, and untruths are not uncovered, it easily becomes a way of life, believing that they might always 'get away with it.'

Perhaps we are able to recall times from our childhood when we were scared to take the blame for something we did, because we feared retribution. We might have blamed a sibling for a broken window, a spilt drink which left a stain on a carpet, a hitting because she/he hit first. There are many examples, insignificant now, but not at the time committed, but because we escaped punishment which was our due, we were encouraged to believe that hiding in lies was worthwhile.

As Christian adults, we hopefully have learnt that lying is totally unacceptable to God. **Proverbs 12:22 Lying lips are an abomination to the Lord, but those who deal truthfully are His delight.**

There are many ways in which we hide ourselves in lies, but each time we do, a little of our soul is damaged, a little of our soul is eaten away, and we carry a heaviness within us. Is it worth not to be honest, even in the smallest of things? Perhaps you were given too much change after purchasing something, and your thoughts were, 'well it was their mistake, and they will hardly miss a few pence.'

Maybe so, but stealing even a few pence is a form of lying. Why risk the stain it makes on your soul? A lie is a lie, no matter what the degree.

The biggest liar of course, is Satan - the Father of lies - and quite often, because of his dulcet tones, we are led to believe him because he comes across as convincing in whatever he is lying about. The best way to avoid believing his lies is to remain constantly in touch with our Saviour who cannot lie, for He is the way, the truth and the life. By walking with Him we can be certain of walking in truth. **John 14:6 I am the way, the truth and the life, no one comes to the Father except through me.**

God gave man a free will, to choose right from wrong, good from evil, truth from lies. Satan lied to deceive Adam into thinking he was telling the truth, thus also hoodwinking Eve.

Lies and disobedience are still with us today, dictated to the world to a large extent by corrupt governments, fake news within modern technology and its abundance of trickery. We have become, in the 21st century, more and more gullible and vulnerable, progressively believing and trusting in untruths.

God sought out Adam and of course Adam owned up, blaming the devil. Nevertheless he was still responsible for his disobedience. Who do we blame? We are accountable for our own wrongdoing.

When we don't want to get up and face another day sometimes, we might hide under the blankets, pretending to feel unwell; perhaps we have hidden behind the garden shed door not wanting to face up to a neighbour, having broken his plants with a football. These might sound very insignificant, feasibly they are, but little things build up and eventually little things become bigger things without us realising it. We need to be aware of our hiding away, take these 'insignificant sins' to the Lord and chat with Him about them – after all He has said that we must become perfect as He is perfect. It doesn't make us 'goody goodies', 'babies' or whatever term one likes to use for a person who lives as righteously as possible, it makes us just that – 'righteous' in the sight of God, and not being concerned with what others think of us, maybe damaging our egos, but hey!

Rudyard Kipling (1865-1936) writes on truth and lies in his famous poem 'If'.

If you can keep your head when all about you
Are losing theirs and blaming it on you,
If you can trust yourself when all men doubt you,
But make allowance for their doubting too;
If you can wait and not be tired by waiting,
Or being lied about, don't deal in lies,
Or being hated, don't give way to hating,
And yet don't look too good, nor talk too wise.
If you can dream – and not make dreams your master;
If you can think – and not make thoughts your aim;
If you can meet with Triumph and Disaster
And treat those two impostors just the same;
If you can bear to hear the truth you've spoken
Twisted by knaves to make a trap for fools,

Or watch the things you gave your life to, broken,
And stoop and build 'em up with worn-out tools;
If you can make one heap of all your winnings
And risk it on one turn of pitch-and-toss,
And lose, and start again at your beginnings
And never breathe a word about your loss;
If you can force your heart and nerve and sinew
To serve your turn long after they are gone,
And so hold on when there is nothing in you
Except the Will which says to them: 'Hold on!'
If you can talk with crowds and keep your virtue,
Or walk with Kings – nor lose the common touch,
If neither foes or loving friends can hurt you,
If all men count with you, but none too much;
If you can fill the unforgiving minute
With sixty seconds' worth of distance run,
Yours is the Earth and everything that's in it,
And – which is more – you'll be a Man, my son!

A great poem and one to take on board for life.

There was a little girl, aged between 8-10 years old, who often used to go after school to her father's office to wait for him to finish his work before going home. It was an pportunity to do her homework, sitting at the other side of his huge desk, where she had plenty of space to lay out the necessary books. One afternoon, she was working on her sums, using her fingers for counting, when she was startled by the sudden appearance of her father's boss. He had been standing behind her for a few seconds. Greeting each other, the gentleman asked the child what she was doing, and having answered 'sums', he took her by surprise and asked if she counted on her fingers. Her reply was an immediate 'No.' She remembers her heart beating faster and a feeling of guilt washing over her. Because she would have felt embarrassed if admitting the truth, she had impulsively lied. But the boss had seen her using her fingers on first entering the room, and though she had discerned this, because of fear, she lied. A 'white lie' maybe, but it affected her, and she never forgot that incident, learning that it is always wrong to lie. In his kindness, the boss didn't rebuke her. He knew that she knew that he knew!

A conscience is given to us by God – it is supposed to keep us safe, honourable and righteous.

Revelation 21:25-27 tells us that liars will not enter the gates of the New Jerusalem, but only those who are written in the Lamb's book of life. Liars are considered defiled.

Let us not look on the matter lightly, for God will not be insulted. After all, He is the great I AM, the Creator of heaven, earth and all that is in them, plus the enormity of His creating man in His own image.

In Acts 5:1-11 we read the story of Ananias and Sapphira who lied to the Holy Spirit. They both fell down dead having done so. That is somewhat scary, but should be an ever reminder in our hearts and minds if we are ever tempted to lie in order to justify our actions. Lying is a form of escape, somewhere we can run to in times of need. But weighing up the consequences, this escape route is really a dead end. We need to run to the Father, our precious Father, who is our hiding place and remain in His everlasting arms of comfort. He will guide us into all truth, and when we suffer from telling the truth in dire circumstances, He will always be with us, for as we honour Him by our truthfulness, so He honours us. As Christians we must rise above the world of lies, teach our children to do the same, and from the very start of their understanding. Playing the 'blame game' is quite prevalent among siblings and when recognised, needs to be handled gently but firmly.

May we always turn to the Lord in trust. He is our hiding place, somewhere warm, comforting and safe. He waits for us to do so, and He will never turn us away.

You are My Hiding Place
You always fill my heart
With songs of deliverance
Whenever I am afraid
I will trust in You.
Let the weak say I am strong
In the strength of the Lord.

Taken from **Psalm 32** – written as a song by Michael Ledner

Jesus was accused of lying. Claiming that He was the Son of God, He was asked to prove this by coming down from the cross. **And those who passed by blasphemed Him, wagging their heads and saying, "Aha! You who destroy the temple and build it in three days, save yourself, and come down from the cross!" Likewise the chief priests also, together with the scribes, mocked and said among themselves, "He saved others; Himself he cannot save. Let Christ, the King of Israel, descend now from the cross, that we may see and believe." And those who were crucified with him reviled Him. Mark 15:29-32.**

Jesus, of course, was telling the truth, but this was beyond those who taunted Him. And in all that, He forgave them, for He said, 'they know not what they do'. Once they realised what they had done, and if the truth came into their hearts, no doubt they would have repented and known His forgiveness. We too are forgiven for our wrong actions. Repentance is always called for and we are washed clean. What a magnificent Saviour we have! **Psalm 51** is a wonderful prayer of repentance, and **verse 6** tells us **Behold, You desire truth in the inward parts, and in the hidden part You will make me to know wisdom.**

Oh yes, we so need wisdom; wisdom which is made up of common sense, insight, understanding and intelligence. True wisdom is not being 'know alls', full of non discretionary knowledge, but true knowledge and inspiration, given to us by the Holy Spirit.

Media lies cause confusion and arguments, disrupting people's lives; conspiracy theories cause scepticism, leaving us with questions as to which or what is false or true. We don't have to listen to these theories, we only have to listen to the voice of the Holy Spirit who is Truth. We are so easily led into thinking that we have to hear what the world believes, but we know what it believes. We must hold on tightly to the Word of God. We cannot live off the media, but we can and must live off His Word, for it alone will sustain us.

A common lie is one that is put on a CV when applying for a job - higher grades than we have, more experience than we have, older in age than we are. The latter was a frequent lie for young men wanting to go to war. Grave yards hold many under age men who were killed in wars. Were their lies justified?

We might exaggerate a situation, causing unnecessary concern to others. Perhaps we want to be thought of as better than we are, so we deliberately give the wrong impression of ourselves. We possibly agree with certain points of view or facts regarding some discussion, so as to come across pleasing to everyone, but outside of their company dispute everything we have agreed to. We are so often afraid of 'losing face', being different, because we have contrasting views and think the only way to be popular or liked is to agree with one and all. But this is cowardly, and only goes to show a flaw in one's character. Honesty always pays and automatically commands respect.

There are people in this world who have claimed to be Christ. They have even appeared on the television stating that lie, and being accompanied by Mary, his mother. How bizarre! It might be that they are seeking attention, but eventually they peter out, for lies do not hold. We know that when we have the Spirit of Truth within us, we are able to discern between lies and truth. **John 16:13. However, when He, the Spirit of truth has come, He will guide you into all truth, for He will not speak on His own authority, but whatever He hears He will speak; and He will tell you things to come.**

Let us not be fearful, for Jesus said this would happen in the last days. **Matthew 24:5 "For many will come in my name, saying, 'I am the Christ,' and will deceive many."**

We tell lies to protect people from harm, believing that it is for their own good, then suddenly one day we find that the 'truth is out' and it brings hurt, which one might surmise as unnecessary. Why hurt someone by telling the truth, when by keeping quiet the person is protected, we query. This needs serious talking through, and because we are defective human beings and not always wise, it is best to ask this question of the One and only sound person we know – Jesus. His advice is the best advice. For us, if we are asked advice on a situation, is - no advice is the best advice!

To keep ourselves as healthy as possible we try and eat well, food that will give us the daily energy we need. That is for our physical being. We also need spiritual food, reminding ourselves that Jesus says that **"Man cannot live on bread alone, but on every word that proceeds from the mouth of God." Matthew 4:4.**

Most of us enjoy food, many having a desire for the real mouth watering, gooey delicacies! But after eating salads, fresh fruit, lean meats and generally healthy cuisine, we feel cleaner within ourselves. Contrasting this with indulging in the naughty fare, we might suffer from discomfort, maybe indigestion and certainly have less energy. When we feed on the Word, our unworldly sustenance, we feel fresh, reinvigorated, and encouraged, so it is important for our sacred well being that we have a daily intake of this spiritual nourishment. And to think that Jesus is feeding us personally – what an honour!

If we are ever tempted to lie, we might be able to plan what to do or say beforehand, which would make it easier, but one can be caught on the spot when a spontaneous lie might well be the outburst. Think back to the little girl – her lie was spontaneous because she was afraid, even though she knew that she had been found out. Being fearful is not a good state of mind, and really there is no need for it.

Psalm 91:2 tells us that we shall abide under the shadow of the Most High, that He is our refuge and fortress and in Him we can trust. Best of all is **verse 4** that tells us that **He will cover you with His feathers and under His wings you shall take refuge. His Truth shall be your shield and buckler…** This tells us that if we abide in Christ, we shall be fine, we shall have that peace that passes all understanding, and know that the truth sets us free.

In **Genesis 20** we read that Abraham lied about Sarah, his wife, saying that she was his sister. One might think *'Abraham, he of all people!'* yes, Abraham, he was just as human as us, thinking he could deceive Abimelech. Why did he lie? Because he was afraid of losing Sarah on account of her beauty. Would you be believe, Isaac did the exact same thing with regard to Rebekah, which is referred to in **Genesis 26!** They both lied due to their fear.

We go on to learn in **Genesis 29** that Laban lied. Isaac and Rebekah had two sons, Esau, the older, and Jacob. When Isaac was old and resting he called to Esau asking to take him his favourite food, that he may eat and bless Esau before he dies. Rebekah was eaves dropping and because Jacob was her favourite son, she told him to disguise himself as his brother when taking in the food and in so doing would receive his father's blessing instead. This lie caused havoc, leading to hatred, threats and resentment. But let us not stop here. We read on and find Laban, Rachel's father, who hires Jacob for an agreed seven years, didn't keep his word, giving Leah in Rebekah's place, and then Jacob had to wait another seven years. **Chapter 31:7 "Yet your father has deceived me, and changed my wages ten times, but God did not allow him to hurt me.....".** Here we see how God protects those who are honest. It would be wothwhile to read up to the end of **Chapter 36,** but of course, it is always beneficial to read further.

Many of us will be familiar with 'The Judas Kiss'. How sad to kiss someone with a deceitful action as Judas did with Jesus. Having arranged with the soldiers to arrest Jesus, **"The one I kiss is the man; arrest him..." Matthew**

26. He was lying to Jesus by his silence and brief kiss, as apparently this was the custom at the time for paying respect to a superior.

The most beautiful and saddest poem, *The Ballad of the Judas Tree* by Ruth Etchells (1931-2012), has to stir the soul to its depths, as it brings to the surface how much Jesus loves those who betray Him.

In Hell there grew a Judas Tree
Where Judas hanged and died
Because he could not bear to see
His master crucified

Our Lord descended into Hell
And found His Judas there
For ever hanging on the tree
Grown from his own despair

So Jesus cut His Judas down
And took him in His arms

"It was for this I came" He said
"And not to do you harm

My Father gave me twelve good men
And all of them I kept
Though one betrayed and one denied
Some fled and others slept

In three days time I must return
To make the others glad
But first I had to come to Hell
And share the death you had

My tree will grow in place of yours
Its roots lie here as well
There is no final victory
Without this soul from Hell"

So when we all condemn him
As of every traitor worst
Remember that of all his men
Our Lord forgave him first.

As is mentioned in the poem there were others who betrayed Him, those with whom we are also familiar. Peter, who loved the Lord dearly, but because of fear, denied that he knew Him. **Luke 22:54-62.** Others ran off, as they were obviously afraid, knowing that they had been seen with Him.

Have you ever thought that you might, at some time, lied to yourself? Perhaps having broken something belonging to a friend or relative you promised to fix it, and never did. You know in your heart that you are absolutely useless at 'fixing' mostly anything; it is not in you, it is not one of your 'gifts'; you are better at breaking rather than fixing! In your pretence, you put the item away in the garage or in a cupboard, saying that you will get round to it as soon as possible. The soon as possible takes a long time, and eventually you forget about it, that is until one day it suddenly appears. Memory clicks in and perhaps guilt. You might think that because so much time has lapsed there is no point in doing anything with it now, just forget it again – or, you could recover it, confess to the person to whom you said you would fix it, admitting honestly that you can't. At the time you felt the need to cover up, to your way of thinking, inadequacies, which you felt belittled by. But, if you had really thought about it, an apology would have been so much easier, and perhaps a replacement or payment would have proved to be more credible.

There was a young man who was afraid of failing his degree at university, so asked a friend if he would sit the required exams in his place. This he did, and successfully passed. The man who 'bunked' applied for a job, filling in the necessary forms and 'proof' of his degree. He was accepted for the position of junior accountant and over a period of thirty years worked for the same company eventually achieving a high position.

Then he came to Christ! It is said that he told those in authority that he had lied his way into the firm all those years ago, and that he was sorry. He left without the salary due to him, lost his pension and took a job selling newspapers. Having given his life to Jesus and repented, he knew he couldn't continue in his bluff. What a downfall and loss of face, but, he was now a man of God, cleansed and forgiven!

No doubt the expression 'to cry wolf' is recognisable to many, which leads to the following very famous poem written by Hilaire Belloc (1870-1953). Matilda who 'cried wolf' and by doing so lost her life.

Matilda Who Told Lies and was Burned to Death.

Matilda told such dreadful lies,
It made one gasp and stretch one's eyes;
Her aunt, who, from her earliest youth,
Had kept a strict regard for truth,
Attempted to believe Matilda:
The effort very nearly killed her,
And would have done so, had not she
Discovered the infirmity.
For once, towards the close of Day,
Matilda, growing tired of play,
And finding she was left alone,
Went tiptoe to the telephone
And summoned the immediate aid
Of London's noble Fire-Brigade.
Within an hour the gallant band
Were pouring in on every hand,
From Putney, Hackney Downs and Bow.

With courage high and hearts a-glow,
They galloped, roaring through the town,
'Matilda's house is burning down!'
Inspired by British cheers and loud
Proceeding from the frenzied crowd,
They ran their ladders through a score
Of windows on the ball room floor;
And took peculiar pains to souse
The pictures up and down the house,
Until Matilda's aunt succeeded
In showing them they were not needed;
And even then she had to pay
To get the men to go away.
It happened that a few weeks later
Her aunt was off to the theatre
To see that interesting play
The Second Mrs. Tanqueray.
She had refused to take her niece
To hear this entertaining piece;
A deprivation just and wise
To punish her for telling lies.

That night a fire did break out -
You should have heard Matilda shout!
You should have heard her scream and bawl,
And throw the window up and call
To people passing in the street -
(The rapidly increasing heat
Encouraging her to obtain
Their confidence) – but in vain!
For every time she shouted 'Fire!'
They only answered 'Little Liar!'
And therefore when her aunt returned,
Matilda, and the house, were burned.

This poem is a fine example of a so called 'fun lie', - well – maybe not so fun as it turned into a disaster!

We must be sensitive to those around us, but at the same time not be 'kill joys'. There are fun lies, ones that can bring about much laughter, and are quite harmless, but discernment is paramount.

A family was travelling along a farm road, out of sight of any house or lodge, when the mother said that she needed a WC. Father pulled into the side of the road, mother got out of the car, looked furtively around before walking further into the bush and behind a tree. One of their children, knowing that she was afraid of cows, and seeing that there weren't any in the vicinity, shouted 'Mind the cows!' Needless to say, mother jumped in fright, leaving herself in an uncomfortable state running back to the car. Fortunately she had a good sense of humour, and though the child was told off, but not seriously, they continued on their journey with much laughter ensuing!

April Fools Day can be a time of fun, though apparently only up to midday. If you make a fool of someone by an untruth, if it is later than 12 noon, then you are the fool!

So we must always differentiate between the fun lies and the serious ones, keeping our sense of humour and remaining honourable.

To end, let us think on a couple of incidences in the Old Testament, which suggest that maybe God put His signature to these particular lies. In the book of Joshua

Chapter 2 we read about Rahab, the prostitute, who willingly hid two spies in the attic of her house. She was questioned about the men and admitted that they had paid her a visit, but were no longer with her, lying by suggesting, when leaving her, the direction they might have travelled. The lie was to protect herself, her family and the men, and through this the Israelites defeated Jericho; she also became a changed woman. (Some scholars believe that she was the great, great, grandmother of King David. However, this is not factual.)

One other incident is in **Exodus 1** where a new king over Egypt was concerned about the growth in population of the Israelites. Torture and affliction did not deter their increase, so he asked the midwives to kill the boy infants. But because the midwives feared God, they didn't obey, and when queried, they lied, saying that the Hebrew women gave birth before the midwives arrived. Thus the children continued to multiply. Nevertheless, God honoured the midwives by blessing them with families of their own.

Both events make for an interesting read, allowing one to capture the whole essence of each situation.

Many will say that it was wrong to tell these lies, that God could have dealt with the situations in some other way; yes, He could have, but He knew the hearts of these people and would have made plans incorporating their lies. Could there be such a thing as 'righteous lying'? If the Almighty is involved in the situation, and one is a highly commendable person, perhaps so. Whatever He says goes and if there is honesty in our hearts, then all has to be well. God respects us, faulty as we are, if we aim to do the right thing, so one would be forgiven for believing that these lies were all part of God's plans for a positive outcome of the dire situation that hung over Israel. They also ultimately brought God the glory.

As always we need to consistently remember that His ways are not our ways, nor His thoughts our thoughts, and bearing this in mind, no matter what, recognise that His ways are the smartest and one hundred percent reliable, whether dealing with great exploits or personal concerns.

And the Lord is the one who goes before you. He will be with you, He will not leave you nor forsake you; do not fear nor be dismayed. Deuteronomy 31:8.

Chapter 12
MY THOUGHTS ARE NOT YOUR THOUGHTS NOR ARE YOUR WAYS MY WAYS

Isaiah 55:8 has once again veined its way through, this time with added attention given to it. It is a very poignant verse, hopefully, eventually penetrating the hearts and minds of its readers. It is often heard quoted, perhaps because it is 'alive' with truth, hope, love, encouragement, smiles and laughter, and so much more.

But let us not neglect the other verses, all coming under the title of "God's Offer of Mercy."

It is an exciting chapter and one which, if no other, should hold our attention every day. In order for it to infiltrate our minds and hearts, we need to focus, so that in the fullness of time, its words will pop into our thinking, not just occasionally, but regularly. Thus it is imperative that we read it habitually, thus creating an on going thought pattern. Quite often one hears people whistling theme tunes from certain TV or radio programmes they listen to, implying that they probably watch or listen to the programme on a frequent, or daily basis. The same applies to reading and praying, though not to become parrot like in our prayers, but in sincerity repeating requests, or better still offering up lots of 'thank yous'!

The chapter 'sings'. It lifts the faith by its invitation from God himself to join Him in celebrating all He has to offer. In **Verse 7,** He even invites the wicked!

He offers us food and drink without payment, asking why we spend our wages on things that will not last. If we heed Him, He will give us the best. He offers us life, honour and glory, so much so that others will come running to us in order to share in our bounty. Everything in our lives will grow and multiply, thereby meeting our needs.

The word that He speaks will not fail to do what He planned for it, as it will do everything that He had planned it to do.

Our joy will be as such – the trees will clap their hands; we will live in peace, surrounded by singing mountains and hills. The thorn and briar will be replaced with smooth and safe, sweet smelling flowers and foliage. All these and more!

When we have learnt to really believe and understand that His ways and thoughts are not the same as ours, we will find our lives so much more peaceful.

There are those folk throughout Scripture who, understanding that His ways and thoughts were different to theirs, also knew *not to lean on their own understanding, but in all their ways acknowledge Him.* Perhaps we can link this **Proverb 3:5-8** with **Isaiah 55:8** - for when we do not try to understand the deep things of God, accepting that His decisions, His plans, His appointments, are far more worthy than ours, then we have reached the pinnacle of our faith; then we can move on like Abraham, David, Mary, the mother of Jesus, Hannah, the mother of Solomon and others. **Hebrews 11** gives us a list of those who looked on God as sovereign. And as we too, in the 21stcentury, look on the Almighty as King, we can receive blessing after blessing from Him.

It is essential that we consult Him before we take on any enormous task, knowing that His ways and thoughts are off line in comparison to ours. And remember as well, no matter how small our requests, problems or concerns, know that our God is available at all times - for He never sleeps or slumbers.

Psalm 121 He will not allow your foot to be moved; He who keeps you will not slumber. Behold, He who keeps Israel shall neither slumber nor sleep.

Chapter 13
CHOOSE TODAY WHOM YOU WILL SERVE

Romans 12:2 And do not be conformed to this world, but be transformed by the renewing of your minds, that you may prove what is that good and acceptable and perfect will of God.

It is crucial for Christians to be aware of what is expected of them as they walk the 'narrow way'. God doesn't compromise on what He expects, and His expectations are all because He loves us. Why would He have gone through the crucifixion if after His last words from the cross **'It is finished' John 19:30** life goes on just as before?

We are called to follow Him, He has chosen us to do so, but on His terms not ours. God has set down conditions and expects us to keep them.

Certain terms and conditions are accredited when we take up employment. If we want to do well, we must be honest and trustworthy; we are paid a salary which we try to spend wisely. We are not 'goody goodies', just righteous citizens wanting to make a positive and clean living. So it is if we want to inherit eternity, we must listen to, and obey God's rules – which are, as we know The Ten Commandments.

Having suffered and died for our sins, Jesus then sent His Holy Spirit to guide us in all that we do. It is wonderful to have a relationship with our Saviour, and the invitation is offered to all. **Mark 2:15-17** tells us where He invites people to follow Him, but in doing so, they have to be prepared to change their way of life. It is still the same today.

Us humans quite often make rules to suit ourselves, to fit in with our way of thinking; we then become selfish and demanding, the devil having whispered furtively into our ears with regard our way of life. He does it mostly through the television and social media, fooling us into thinking that everything and anything goes. As Frank Sinatra sings, 'I Did It My Way', and wasn't he, in this song, and are not we, proud of doing things our way?

The digital world came forth surreptitiously, taking all peoples of the earth into a world of mistrust and havoc, with devastating harm thrust on us all, and mainly because of its misuse, obviously organised by the evil one, which blinds us into saying, "Well, everybody uses their smart phones everywhere and anywhere they want, even in church; it has a Bible so we can follow everything on it, what's the problem? How, is the question, can anyone centre their full attention on the service? We are very easily distracted, and there is no doubt that texts come through, messages and silent phone calls, which are all an intrusion creating a diversion. The reason for going to church is to honour God, to keep the Sabbath holy, plus we are able to spend time together in praise, worship, to listen and hear God's word – without worldly distractions. We have to choose whom we will serve. **Joshua 24:15 Choose this day whom you will serve.**

Joshua 24:1-33. (Recommended to read) We must put away our foreign gods, serve Jehovah, the one true God and obey Him only. It is as simple as that.

The digital gadgets with which so many are enamoured, were initially intended for good use, perhaps, but someone else, who always hovers in the background in the spiritual world, had different plans, plans to distract us, perhaps like the golden calf at the time of Moses. Is that a phoney suggestion? It is out of tune with modern society, but then so is Christianity - real Christianity.

We must know and recognise that Satan is a liar, a great voice impersonator, and if we are not walking closely with the Lord, we hear his lying dulcet tones and are taken in. Because advance science is so very clever and appealing, insisting that what is on offer are 'must haves' we are so easily beguiled. It, no doubt, is here to stay, but we need to have wisdom as to its usage. This has already been mentioned, but because it is so vital, it necessitates repetition.

Exodus 32 tells us of Aaron agreeing to the making of the golden calf at the Israelites request whilst Moses was on the mountain of Sinai meeting with God. They were bored and wanted something to do. They were a faithless and 'stiff necked' people. Are we the same in wanting to please ourselves with our heads constantly down and our fingers continually tapping? One can imagine when Jesus appears at His second coming, no one will see Him because of their digital god – heads bowed, otherwise occupied (not in prayer) instead of being upright, waiting for that wonderful day. 1Thessalonianss 5 tells us about the day of the Lord's coming. **For you yourselves know perfectly that the day of the Lord comes as a thief in the night.** We have to be on watch all the time – no slacking or sleeping, heads up, being aware.

Mobile phones have become embodied in our every day life in such a way that they are part of our 'dress'; they are thrust into babies hands before they are able to talk, walk or read. We need to look up and pay attention to what is happening around us, let alone allowing these phones to interrupt our worship. God has stipulated that He will not have any other gods before Him; this He makes abundantly clear in the Old Testament, as He does in the New. We are not to 'love' our smart phones, they are simply to be used as a tool with which to make genuine and helpful contacts - outside our time of worship and all Christian gatherings. How we use them in our private lives is also up for question, but in this let us use common sense.

Come out from among them, and be separate, says the Lord. Do not touch what is unclean, and I will receive you. 2 Corinthians 6:17-18. One might ask if the smart phone is considered to be 'unclean'. In many aspects, yes, it is. When we are in the presence of God, if we believe that He is holy, then it has to be. Moses and Joshua were both asked to take off their sandals as they were standing on holy ground; are we not standing on holy ground when we meet with the Lord? It really is audacious to hold onto our phones when we are in His company.

Be holy, for I am holy, Jesus says in 1 Peter 1:16. This is not just a statement, it is a command. How can we be holy when we have a constant hold of our smart phones in church, Bible study and prayer group? They are a distraction, they are a bluff. They keep us separated from God and joined to the world. We are to be detached from the world, keeping our eyes on Jesus, not on anything else, particularly when we set time aside to be with Him. Of course we have free wills, so it is our decision whether or not to use the phone in church. It is bad enough everywhere else – the cinema, during meal times, meetings, whilst shopping, walking, crossing he road, during conversations, in the bathroom, the bedroom, outside the school gate where children are ignored and left feeling unimportant. We need to discipline ourselves, principally in church, where this gadget is not necessary. We have God's Word, the Bible; we have hymn books, though for many years, the overhead projector has been used. Out with the old and in with the new is a constant. We tire easily and become bored, instead of valuing that which is God given, and being content with that which is satisfactory. We are fickle and like the chameleon, forever changing our colours to suit whatever we want or are told by the world that we 'must have'. We are so easily influenced by the world, believing all what it tells us.

Mobile phones do have a worthwhile part to play in society today, but again, to emphasise, we must be discerning as to their use and keep a healthy and respectful balance, which overall, is missing. We need to learn to ignore the 'must have' attitude which is propelled upon us. Jesus laid down His life for us, let us lay down our smart phones for Him. It is the least we can do. Apart from being a distraction in our churches, we are being extremely rude. Let us think for a moment of how we would feel if whilst sharing something with a friend, and she/he started texting, reading a text, or answering a call? It would be the height of bad manners. It is the height of bad manners. 'Manners maketh man' an Eton school principle back in the 16th century named William Hormon, advocated. Eton or Comprehensive makes no difference! And in the Victorian era, children were not permitted to speak unless spoken to. An extremely strict rule, but adhered to, though we might say today, quite cruel. (Unfortunately, society has gone too far over the other way.) But it is not a stricture or cruel, to not use our phones when in the presence of our Lord, when we have invited Him to be with us by His Holy Spirit. It is not only a discipline we should adhere to, but should want.

Perhaps the reader will be thinking that surely this is going over the top of what is expected of us. If we have children let us think of what we expect of them. We hopefully teach them ground rules, which we trust they will abide by. We confidently set good examples of behaviour and anything which is ignored there is a punishment. How did God punish the Israelites after they were found to have made the golden calf as a god? It was dreadful - the whole scenario can be found in Exodus 32 where we read that God threatened disaster to come upon them. But Moses, angry as well, and understanding God's wrath, pleaded with Him not to destroy them, reminding Him of His promises. Moses would have given his own life just to spare them! That was quite something. Is there anyone we know who would do the same for us? Is God angry with us? Do we ever think about that or ask ourselves these questions?

Ah! Jesus gave His life to spare us from God's wrath, He took it all on the cross. Nevertheless we must still work out our own salvation, living in righteousness and obedience.

The fear of the Lord is the beginning of wisdom; a good understanding have all those who do His commandments. His praise endures for ever. Psalm 111:10.

Is it really that big of a deal not to use our smart phones in church, Bible study and prayer group? One would think it would be refreshing to let them go for even a little while. It seems we do not tire of its ever presence, the demands it makes on our lives and our demands on it. It appears to be like having a dog snapping at our heels, forever clamouring for attention, no let up until seen to. We need to train this 'snapper' and turn our hearts, minds and souls 100% to the Living Lord, to really love Him, not just in words, but in Truth. We need to be true to ourselves, remembering WHO he is.

By switching off our phones, primarily when in His presence, (though at other times it wouldn't hurt to do so) would be like removing our sandals, for we are on holy ground, and thus we honour Him who will honour us. **1 Samuel 2:30** tells us **"….for those who honour me I will honour and those who despise me shall be lightly esteemed."**

Psalm 8:4-5 When I consider your heavens, the work of your hands and of your fingers, the moon and the stars which you have ordained, what is man that you are mindful of him, and the son of man that you visit him? For you have made him a little lower than the angels, and you have crowned him with glory and honour.

Mary Marriot

Chapter 14
THERE IS SOMETHING VERY SERIOUSLY WRONG

Most of us don't like to deliberately hurt anyone. We are usually sensitive to another's feelings and so avoid hurting them. However, there are times this proves to be unavoidable, and the knife, metaphorically speaking of course, is plunged in. The outcome can be devastating or healing, depending on the circumstances and who and what is involved.

Do we ever think that we may hurt God? Is this a ridiculous question? Well, one might think so, but it is a question needed to be asked and then answered, and answered truthfully. It is so easy to wave aside bothering feelings that might sear our conscience at times. In fact they are easy to discard with one brush off and a replacement thought or concern.

Perhaps we find compromising quite difficult, again depending on what. But to compromise on God's word is an absolute no, no. There has to be absolutely no compromise with God's word. There is no black and white to think about, it is just as it is – the whole truth and nothing but the truth. If we don't like it, then the best thing to do is wrap ourselves up and go elsewhere. In **John 6** under the title 'Many Disciples Turn Away', Jesus having told them about eating His body and drinking His blood, **Verse 53.** They were horrified at this thought, saying **"This is a hard saying, who can understand it?" Verse 60.** When some of the disciples walked away, Jesus turned to the twelve asking if they too wanted to walk away. Peter answered **"Lord, to whom shall we go? You have the words of eternal life." Verse 68.** So it is with us – we either walk away or are prepared to walk along the restricted path with Him who offers eternal life.

Is this harsh? Not really. In this materialistic world we go along with all sorts of dictates, some of which we agree on, others not. We have a choice. But in God's world, we do not have such freedom of choice. We must be aware that if we choose to follow Him along the narrow way, there will be no compromise on the journey. No either or, buts or ifs, maybe or maybe not; it is what it is. "Follow Me," says Jesus to the fisherman – yes or no? If the answer is yes, we have to drop our 'nets' without hesitation and walk with Him on the non compromise road.

Human nature dictates that we are selfish. Fortunately many of us have unselfish genes, which make us reasonable people. Self preservation is quite natural, and yet there are those who give their lives in order not to compromise – many for their faith. We just have to look to the saints of old, and modern. Being burnt to death at the stake would make one really think about denying one's beliefs – just the thought of such a horrific death makes one recoil. If we are asked to denounce certain truths, do we compromise with the thought - 'it's okay, God understands these terrible circumstances, He knows my heart, so He will forgive me.' Yes, He is an all forgiving God, and as we know Jesus took all the punishment for our transgressions; He also understands our fears. However, this is not about whether we deny our faith, but compromising it, twisting it to meet man's wishes using the 'love of God' as an excuse to do what we want to do.

This brings us to the point in acknowledging that there is something very seriously wrong within the Body of Christ. We have become 'man pleasers', being ill at ease with certain truths in the Bible. It is to our peril if this continues, and we need to search out our hearts very deeply and earnestly.

1 Thessalonians 2:4 But just as we have been approved by God to be entrusted with the gospel, so we speak, not as pleasing men, but God who examines our hearts.

Luke 16:15 And He said to them, "You are those who justify yourselves in the sight of men, but God knows your hearts; for that which is highly esteemed among men is detestable in the sight of God."

We need to still ourselves. Life is so loud, so busy, we have joined the mayhem of the world, instead of setting ourselves apart as followers of Christ. We need to be still and know that HE IS GOD; He is the great I AM and He is a HOLY GOD, telling us to 'Be holy, for I am holy.'

Holiness is us walking in obedience, being of 'the same mind' as each other. And He must come first in our lives – the 1st Commandment is to love Him with all our hearts, our minds and our strength, and there must not be any other gods beside Him. A lot to think on, a lot to check out in our Bibles, a lot to pray about.

Philippines 2:2 Then make my joy complete by being like-minded, having the same love, being one in spirit and of one mind.

We are walking a tight rope when we compromise God's Word. Let us be alert to this. There is no middle ground in what we are asked to do, to believe and act. We are losing our balance, and can so easily plunge ourselves and others into the abyss of hell. Why do it just to be popular, just to be liked and thought well of as 'broad minded Christians'?

Jesus never compromised – He said how it was, whether people liked it or not, and we know He was very unpopular with many. He offered eternal life, and He still offers it, but there are conditions attached.

There are 'Ifs' - one of many we find in **Chronicles 7:14. IF my people, who are called by my name will humble themselves, and pray, and seek my face, and turn from their wicked ways; then I will hear from heaven and heal their land.**

Mark 11:25-26 "And whenever you stand praying, IF you have anything against anyone, forgive him, that your Father in heaven may also forgive you your trespasses. But IF you do not forgive, neither will your Father who is in heaven forgive your trespasses."

Christians are opposing Christians in their beliefs. This is absolute nonsense and quite frightening. We have to take our eyes off public opinion and allow God His rightful place. Just because the world now gives an okay to certain aspects of life, which in God's eyes are wrong, why trade-off our own belief and faith by going along with them? True Christians suffer for their faith in many areas, not only because they love their Saviour, but they want to be with Him in heaven. Why put our souls in jeopardy just to be popular? Jesus lost face – and for us. We should be able to lose face for Him.

Followers of Jesus were, and still are, called to tell the Gospel. There is so much talk on 'saving the planet' what is happening to the 'saving of souls'? We are responsible for spreading the Gospel, and having done so, if folk are not interested, do as suggested in **Matthew 10:14 And whoever will not receive you nor hear your words, when you depart from that house or city, shake off the dust from your feet.** At least you will have done your duty. As for 'saving the planet', well, it is a bit late for that! We should have taken more care a long time ago, and though it is still a good thing to care, let us keep in mind that when Jesus comes again, this earth will be done away with and there will be a new one – and a new heaven! So rather than waste breath shouting about saving the planet, we need to shout about saving souls.

Let us remember the words of Jesus in **Matthew 7:22 Many will say to Me in that day, 'Lord, Lord, have we not prophesied in Your name, cast out demons in Your** name, and done many wonders in Your name? What will his reply be? '**I never knew you, depart from me, you who practice lawlessness.**'

There is no denying God's sovereignty; we need to respect it, honour it and believe it. **Those who honour me, I will honour, but those who despise me will be disdained. 1 Samuel 2:30.**

We cannot fool God; we cannot pull the wool over His eyes, so let us not deceive ourselves into thinking that we can. The Bible is the sacred Word of God, and if we misshape it to meet our wanton ways, we will suffer the consequences. He loves mankind, but hates the sin. Why compromise by saying that because He is a loving and all forgiving, merciful and understanding God, so anything goes? He is all these, but let us not use them as an excuse to do what we think is all right to do. When Mary Magdalene was caught in the act of adultery, Jesus told her 'to go and sin no more.'

We need to take our eyes off the things of the world and allow God His rightful place.

Psalm 139: 23-24 Search me, O God and know my heart. Try me, and know my anxieties; And see if there is any wicked way in me, And lead me in the way everlasting.

In order not to agree to differ with regard to the teachings of Scripture, as Paul claims, we must be of 'one mind', and he repeats this in his epistles. Repetition is wanting to make quite clear, that which is considered to be important and necessary.

Philippines 2:2 fulfil my joy by being like-minded, having the same love, being of one accord of one mind.

And in 1Corinthians 10 he is very explicit – Now I plead with you, brethren, by the name of our Lord Jesus Christ, that you all speak the same thing, and that there be no divisions among you, but that you be perfectly joined together in the same mind and in the same judgement. It appears the 'pleading' is still relevant today!

1Peter 3:8 ...all of you be of one mind, having compassion for one another; love as brothers, be tender-hearted, be courteous.

Many might prefer to comply with those who hold some authority as to the teachings of the church, but in having this preference we lose our strength and God's grace to hold on.

IRELAND BEAUTEOUS IRELAND

Ireland beauteous Ireland
What have you done?
You've lost your Christian values
And the devil seems has won.
You've given your soul to Satan,
He laughs at you with glee,
For now you're in his prison
When once you were so free.
Christ gave His life

That you may live
In holiness and love,
Oh Ireland, beauteous Ireland
Return to Him above
Turn back your face toward Him
You'll find He loves you still,
All you need to do now
Is to follow in His will.
The world and all its offerings
Is just a passing through,
But a new life of repentance
Is what Jesus offers you.
Renew your soul, your mind, your heart,
He is waiting patiently
So hurry now, don't delay,
For He's lingering anxiously.

Don't hesitate or you'll be lost
It isn't time you have,
Wake up, wake up before too late,

Get out of Satan's grasp.
The Land of Saints and Scholars once,
Such dignity you held,
Now living, dying in your sin,
Quick, hurry leave the world.
Leave the world of sin and shame
And to all that it aspires,
You cannot take it with you,
Know Satan whispers lies.
Jesus is Truth, Life and the Way,
The path to Him is narrow,
The style of life you live right now
Is shot with Satan's arrow.
Ireland beauteous Ireland
A land that once was free.
Repentance is the key word
Go down on bended knee.
Once you have repented
There is no turning back,
Know that all's forgiven.
Hallelujah, welcome back.

There is no atonement,
For this He did for you
That day He hung upon the cross,
He did for all of you.

When a precious soul comes into faith, an invisible veil drops off their spirit. This veil was a cover to keep the person from knowing the truth, the real truth which sets us free to believe that the Scriptures are the uncompromising Word of God.

Kimberly Williams a Christian lady wrote an article in 2007, asking 'Was Jesus Dogmatic?' (She wrote it because she was accused of being so.) It makes for an interesting read, concluding with the following: *"Therefore, if my beliefs are fixed upon the Word of God and Christ Himself than call me dogmatic, call me narrow, call me rigid, call me unending, call me inflexible.* I'll consider it a compliment." This attitude is standing on the Word of God, no compromising, simply accepting the teachings of Jesus Himself, and those He imparted to His apostles.

Values and morals have been depleted in nations that were once Christian, teaching the Ten Commandments and upholding all that is righteous in the sight of God. Of course we fail, but God doesn't look at failures, he looks at righteousness, that which we have lost, because we are made righteous through Jesus. **Romans 3:21-26 and Romans 4:5-8.** If we don't have Jesus, we don't have His righteousness. Our morals and values are valueless.

As true Christians we must hold fast to biblical teachings, not distorting them to suit ourselves, but to respect the truths which they convey and uphold them by our faithfulness to God.

Romans 4:5-8 But to him who does not work but believes on Him who justified the ungodly, his faith is accounted for righteousness, just as David also describes the blessedness of the man to whom God imputes righteousness apart from works. Blessed are those whose lawless deeds are forgiven, and whose sins are covered; Blessed is the man to whom the Lord shall not impute sin.

www.ingramcontent.com/pod-product-compliance
Lightning Source LLC
Chambersburg PA
CBHW050255120526
44590CB00016B/2363